# Uxmal: The History of the Ancient Mayan City

## By Jesse Harasta and Charles River Editors

Picture of the ruins of Uxmal taken by Fernando Tomás

## About Charles River Editors

**Charles River Editors** provides superior editing and original writing services across the digital publishing industry, with the expertise to create digital content for publishers across a vast range of subject matter. In addition to providing original digital content for third party publishers, we also republish civilization's greatest literary works, bringing them to new generations of readers via ebooks.

Sign up here to receive updates about free books as we publish them, and visit Our Kindle Author Page to browse today's free promotions and our most recently published Kindle titles.

# Introduction

**Palimp Sesto's picture of the ruins of Uxmal**

## Uxmal

Many ancient civilizations have influenced and inspired people in the 21st century. The Greeks and Romans continue to fascinate the West today. But of all the world's civilizations, none have intrigued people more than the Mayans, whose culture, astronomy, language, and mysterious disappearance all continue to captivate people. In 2012 especially, there was a renewed focus on the Mayans, whose advanced calendar has led many to speculate the world would end on the same date the Mayan calendar ends, but if anything, the focus on the "doomsday" scenario overshadowed the Mayans' true contribution to astronomy, language, sports, and art.

The Maya maintained power in the Yucatan for over a thousand years, and in the late stages of the "Classical" era (3rd-9th centuries AD), the city of Uxmal was one of its most noteworthy places. While it was not as powerful as cities like Tikal, Uxmal was apparently at the forefront of Mayan culture, particularly when it came to architecture. However, while Uxmal used high ground to display its prominence, and the ruins are still among the most popular places for tourists in the region, the site is still shrouded in mystery. Even as scholars continue to work on the site to further interpret it, it's still unclear when exactly Uxmal was founded, how many people called it home, and when it was abandoned, despite the existence of Mayan chronicles and oral legends.

What is apparent, however, is the skills of Uxmal's artisans, whether through constructing structures like the 5 level Pyramid of Magicians and the expansive Governor's Palace or adorning the structures with precisely detailed art and sculptures. In fact, the craftsmanship can be credited with helping to preserve Uxmal itself.

*Uxmal: The History of the Ancient Mayan City* covers the history of the city, as well as the speculation and debate surrounding it. Along with pictures and a bibliography, you will learn about Uxmal like you never have before, in no time at all.

Tikal: The History of the Ancient Maya's Famous Capital

About Charles River Editors

Introduction

**A Note on the Periods of Mayan History**

This book follows the traditional system of dividing Mayan history into "periods." Much like European history is divided between the Ancient and Medieval Periods based on whether the Roman Empire had fallen or not, there is a great dividing line in Mayan history called the Classic or Postclassic period.

The apogee of Mayan culture and influence was in the period known to Mesoamerican scholars as the "Classical" period. Ranging from to the 3rd-9th centuries, during this time the region was dominated by two great powers, Tikal and Calakmul, located far to the south of the Yucatán in the northern Highlands. This was the era in which Uxmal sprang up as a city in its own right. Meanwhile, to the west, central Mexico was dominated by the cities of Teotihuacan, Cholula and Monte Albán. This was a period of relative stability, though it probably didn't feel that way as the ruling dynasties of Tikal and Calakmul vied for power and fought numerous proxy wars through their many client states . This period is comparable to the great "cold war" between Athens and Sparta in ancient Greece.

Much like the Roman Empire did not collapse in every area at the same time, the change from the Classic to Postclassic occurred in different places differentially. The Classic Mayan world included a constellation of city-states arranged in great, rival, shifting confederacies. These cities, including the famous centers of Tikal, Palenque, Caracol, and Calakmul, were ruled by kings who were considered semi-divine and were widely commemorated in stone monuments. Eventually, however, the great cities of the Classic Period collapsed, one by one. Far from vanishing, Mayan culture persisted, especially in rural areas, and over time, a new series of cities emerged. While the greatest Classic cities were based in the Highlands of modern Mexico and Guatemala, the Postclassic cities, including Chichén Itzá and Mayapán, emerged in the north in the Yucatan peninsula. Generally speaking, the Postclassic period lasted from the 900s until the arrival of the Spanish in the 1500s.

**A Note on Pronunciations and Names**

While the Ancient Maya certainly had their own system of writing, the Spanish Conquest ultimately eradicated knowledge of it, so the Mayan languages have been written for almost 500 years using Latin characters adopted from Spanish by missionary priests. Nonetheless, some of the sounds in the Mayan languages do not correspond directly to sounds in English or Spanish, so some guidance is needed for proper pronunciation.

"X" is pronounced as "SH" so the Mayan city of Yaxchilan is pronounced "Ya-sh-i-laan"

"J" is pronounced as a hard "H" so the Mayan name Jasaw is pronounced "Ha-saw"

"Z" is pronounced like an English "S"

"HU" and "UH" are pronounced like a "W" so the Mexican name Teotihuacán is pronounced "Teo-ti-wa-caan"

The Mayan orthography also uses an apostrophe ( ' ) to mark a sound that does not appear in most European languages called a glottal stop. This represents a stoppage of air in the throat, a bit like the swallowing of the "TT" in "LITTLE" when pronounced by a Cockney Englishman (which would be written in Mayan orthography as: "li'le"). The glotttal stop is considered to be a consonant.

As scholars have increasingly learned to read the sophisticated writing system left behind by the Maya, they have gained a more subtle understanding of their naming practices. Generally speaking, only the names of kings and queens, as well as a few other individuals, are named in the records, and early archaeologists used names that described the name glyphs, with names like "Stormy Sky," "Curl Snout" or "Great Jaguar Paw." Today it's possible to reconstruct the actual sounds of names like Siyaj Chan K'awiil II , Yax Nuun Ayiin I, or Chak Tok Ich'aak I, but these names are quite long and contain many repetitive elements (much like the continual repetition of the names George and Edward among English kings).

**A jade statue depicting Jasaw Chan K'awiil I**

The name Uxmal is pronounced "Ush - Maahl" and the name has a Mayan root: "thrice-built." Unlike the names of some Mayan cities ("Tikal" was probably called "Yax Mutal" by its residents), this is quite probably the original name of the city. That said, the exact reason behind the name is obscured by history, but it has been argued to refer to the central Temple of the Magician, which contains three earlier, smaller temples within it.[1]

---

1   http://yucatan.for91days.com/uxmal-thrice-built-home-of-the-dwarf-king/

# Chapter 1: Description of the Site

**A picture of the front of the Governor's Palace**

"We took another road, and, emerging suddenly from the woods, to my astonishment came at once upon a large open field strewed with mounds of ruins, and vast buildings on terraces, and pyramidal structures, grand and in good preservation, richly ornamented, without a bush to obstruct the view, and in picturesque effect almost equal to the ruins of Thebes...The place of which I am now speaking was beyond all doubt once a large, populous, and highly civilized city. Who built it, why is was located away from water or any of those natural advantages which have determined the sites of cities whose histories are known, what led to its abandonment and destruction, no man can tell." - John Lloyd Stephens, *Incidents of Travel in Central America, Chiapas & Yucatán*, 1843[2]

The city of Uxmal, which once housed an estimated 20,000 people in its urban core and many thousands of others in peripheral farms and vassal cities, is the northernmost of the Puuc city-states that thrived for several centuries in the northern Yucatán Peninsula beginning around the 800s. Uxmal is a majestic city even in its modern ruined form, dominating the landscape from its position atop the Puuc and looking out over the great wide plain of the Yucatán jungle. From atop its pyramids, its ancient rulers must have been able to see much of their kingdom.

---

2   Quoted in: "Uxmal" at *MayanRuins.com* accessed online at: http://mayaruins.com/uxmal01.html

While Uxmal would eventually be superseded in economic and political might by the lowland cities of Chichén Itzá and Mayapán, it would maintain its stately glory long after the city's arrival on the scene and even become a venerated dowager empress to these later cities. Even after its abandonment, the Maya continued to come to its ruins for ceremonial purposes, and their noble families proudly traced their ancestry back to its halls. .

Like all Mayan cities, Uxmal is built around a ceremonial core centered on temples[3], and in Uxmal, this core was built along a north-south axis and was roughly 100,000 square feet (30,000 square meters) in size. The core's social role is comparable to the Westminster area of London: large buildings for administration, housing royals, religious worship and large public gatherings and celebrations[4]. That said, one of the major differences between Uxmal and its southern Classical precursors is that the monumental architecture dominating the city's core is not focused upon the entombment and veneration of dead monarchs but is instead focused upon facilities for the use of the living. In other words, the broad plazas before the tomb-pyramids (such as the central plaza of Tikal) was replaced as the city focal point by grand halls and palaces around central courtyards in Uxmal[5].

The most famous structure in Uxmal is probably the "Pyramid of the Magician," a name that comes from the Spanish "Pirámide del adivino" (which is probably better translated as the Pyramid of the "Diviner" or "Soothsayer"). Rising 115 feet (35 meters), it is crowned by a temple, but unlike all other Mesoamerican pyramids, the base of this structure is elliptical in shape, with the longest measurements of its sides being 280 feet (85 meters) by 165 feet (50 meters).

The Pyramid has five chambers that are traditionally considered to be temples and which archaeologists have numbered using Roman Numerals. Temple V sits at the crown and is called the House of the Magician,[6] and it is known for its impressive latticework panels. Just below it on the structure is Temple IV, which was far more sumptuous in its décor compared to the relative austerity of Temple V. The gate to Temple IV was enormous and covered in zoomorphic masks, geometric patterns and statuary. Since the entrance to Temple V was not visible from the ground, but Temple IV was, it was probable that IV was the central public space of worship[7]. From a distance, as a visitor ascends towards Temple IV, the facade looms above him or her and appears to be the maw of some terrible monster, and it is only when the visitor reaches the top that the complex patterns of statuary and carving separate from one another[8].

---

3  A three dimensional tour of the reconstructed ruins can be found here: http://www.uxmal-3d.com/
4  Pohl (1999). Pgs 108 - 109
5  Pohl (1999). Pg 106
6  These names in Spanish and English were assigned to the sites long after their fall and have no relationship to the original Mayan uses of the sites. The House of the Magician was probably named in a pique of romantic drama as the house seemed to float dramatically above the canopy.
7  For an image of the two entrances visit: http://academic.reed.edu/uxmal/galleries/Mid/Uxmal/Magician/Uxmal-Magician-6.htm
8  Pohl (1999). Pg 110

This face has been argued to be the creator god Itzamna[9], who is sometimes depicted as a great serpent[10].

9   "Uxmal Temple of the Magician" accessed online at: http://inneroptics.net/mayan_kingdom_book/uxmal/
10  "Itzamna" at the *Mythology Dictionary* (2012). Accessed online at: http://www.mythologydictionary.com/itzamna-mythology.html

**Pictures of the Pyramid of the Magician**

**Map of the layout of the Pyramid of the Magician**

As that description suggests, the Pyramid of the Magician demonstrates that Uxmal fused a number of architectural styles as it was seeking its own aesthetic (what would eventually become the Puuc Style, detailed below). The ornate Temple IV is in a more Classical, southern style called Chenes, while the simpler Temple V is in a local Puuc style[11].

To the south of the Pyramid of the Magician is the "Governor's Palace," or the "House of the Governor," which is sometimes considered to be the greatest masterpiece of Mayan architecture. The Palace, which was almost certainly a royal palace, is the largest building in Uxmal and is built on a platform that was located atop another platform (48 feet, 15 meter tall). The Palace is built with a simple, harmonious plan: a long central building flanked by two smaller structures joined to it by roofed arcades. The three buildings share a roof line and are joined together by sharing their raised dais, with a single central staircase.

The compound also had a facade decoration of remarkable contrast. The lower exterior walls, up until a little over the tops of the 13 identical doorways, were covered in smooth, undecorated stucco, but above this is the decorative cornice, a massive carved surface covered in images of ancestors, deities (especially Chaak the rain god), and elaborate geometrical images. Each panel was undoubtedly a work of art comparable to the famous friezes of the Parthenon in Athens (now on display in London). Visitors approaching the central staircase finds these friezes to be particularly impressive because the building has a feature called a "negative batter," meaning that the front walls lean forward. In fact, the base of the facade is close to two feet further from the front staircase than the crest of the frieze. The effect of this carefully planned feature is that the friezes appear to soar overhead, giving additional drama to the structure. The interior of the structure was similarly dramatic, with high vaulted arches and broad paved rooms[12].

11 Pohl (1999). Pg 110
12 Pohl (1999). Pgs 112 - 113

**Pictures of the Governor's Palace**

In front of the House of the Governor is a broad plaza, and on the far side is a worn stone throne carved in the shape of a two-headed jaguar. If one was to stand in the center of the House of the Governor and look directly toward the throne, in a straight line beyond it would be the main pyramid of the vassal city of Kabah. The two-headed jaguar throne appears to have been a symbol of the city since it appears in stone carvings, including one of the only known king, Lord Chak.

Picture of the stone throne

**Pictures of the Great Pyramid**

**Sculptures atop the temple on the Great Pyramid**

The other large structure within the ceremonial center (which has a number of smaller temples, ceremonial ballcourts and elite residential complexes) is called the Nunnery Quadrangle, due to its similarity to a Spanish cloister. This is believed to have been the home of one of the city's elite families and is the grandest of numerous palaces in the city. The complex has four buildings surrounding a central plaza, and it is located almost at the feet of the Pyramid of the Magician. Each of the four buildings is distinct as well. For example, the North is the largest and is 330 feet (100 meters) long and 23 feet (7 meters) high, with friezes that mimic a number of the themes found in the Palace of the Governors. The West building is elaborately decorated with images of the great Central Mexican and Chichén Itzá god Kukulkán the feathered serpent and the earth god Pawahtun. The East building is far less grand but has two-headed serpent carvings, while the friezes of the South building have depictions of miniature houses and mask panels. Archaeologists have argued that the iconography of the North building is associated with the heavens, the West building with the earth, and the South building with the underworld. The East building is still being interpreted[13].

---

13 Pohl (1999). Pgs 111 - 112

The North Building

**The East Building**

The South Building and West Building

**A feathered serpent engraved on the West Building**

While often overlooked by tourists and even many archaeologists, the bulk of the city of Uxmal is found not it the impressive buildings of the ceremonial core but in the residential neighborhoods that sprawl outwards from it. After all, it was here the the vast majority of the citizenry lived and worked, and like all Maya cities, Uxmal was strongly divided between a small elite and a massive laboring class beneath them.

Of course, the residential homes reflect this division. The simplest form of housing was (and in many areas of the rural Yucatán still is) the "pole-and-thatch" style. In this type of home, the builder creates a wooden framework based around four corner poles, and once this framework is in place, outer walls are constructed by lashing horizontal poles between the uprights at the top and bottom and then creating a fence of thin branches between them. The resulting home is only semi-enclosed, so while visitors cannot see in, residents can see out, and breezes waft through the building to keep down the often-oppressive heat. The roof of the home is made of thatching, and the floor of the hut is made of pounded earth which can be easily kept clean by sweeping.

While central buildings like the Pyramid of the Magician or the Governor's Palace were most certainly planned formally by professional architects, the vernacular architecture of the common Maya home was built in a more piecemeal fashion. Generally speaking, buildings were constructed around a central courtyard that included space for gardens, perhaps pens for turkeys, a cistern full of wáter, and outbuildings like a kitchen (separated to prevent losses from cooking fires and to keep the main home cool) and a washroom (the Maya are fastidiously clean and sometimes bath several times a day). As the extended family grew, new rooms might be added to the perimeter of the courtyard, including separate sleeping rooms for unmarried children, new bedrooms for recently-married couples, and other storage rooms. Pole-and-thatch would eventually be replaced if the family had enough wealth to build stone walls, so a family compound may have a combination of wooden and stone buildings.

As might be expected, the stuccoed white stone homes had several advantages over their wooden predecessors. Among other advantages, they did not blow away during the periodic hurricanes, they were safer from thieves, they remained cooler than the outside, and they were a symbol of the family's status. That said, even within stone construction, there was a wide variety of stones of varying qualities, as well as a wide range in proficiency among the carvers and masons, meaning that not all stone construction was equally prestigious. As a result, it was possible for very wealthy individuals to demonstrate their status through the construction of stunning buildings made of exceptional stone, both in size and level of quality[14].

Even the homes of elites had a number of similarities to those of the commoners. As was described above in the Nunnery Quadrangle, the wealthy also had homes built around central courtyards with numerous rooms facing inwards, but of course, the Nunnery also demonstrated the differences between common housing and the finest of the Uxmal palaces. For example, the Nunnery had paved floors both within the houses and in the courtyard itself, as well as a prestigious raised platform or terrace upon which the entire complex was constructed, stone roofs with vaulted arches, and elaborately decorated exteriors and interiors. Where the commoners' homes enjoyed both privacy from the exterior and the ability to look out through the loosely woven walls, the elites achieved the same effect by having stonecarvers make them elaborate limestone latticework for their walls. These elites put great effort into their homes, which appear not only to be constructed for comfort but also to be able to both host and inspire awe in large numbers of guests. The ruling class' culture in Uxmal under the rule of their council appears to

---

14 "People who Lived in Stone Houses: Local Knowledge and Social Difference in the Classic Maya Pucc Region of Yucatan, Mexico" by Kelli Carmean, Patricia A. McAnany and Jeremy A. Sabloff (2011). In the journal *Latin American Antiquity* Vo 22, No 2, Pp 143 - 158

have become a world of sophisticated courtly intrigue involving rival families and a need to entertain on a grand scale. The grandees of Renaissance Venice would have instantly recognized the interplay between politics and socialization that played out in these grand homes.

## Chapter 2: Daily Life in Uxmal

After exploring the ruined homes of commoners and elites, visitors are left with all kinds of burning questions. What was daily life like for these people? How did they go about the events, big and small, that marked their lives? Archaeology can tell visitors much about architecture and provide insights into economic life, but it often stumbles when faced with more intangible questions and figuring out some of the more fragile parts of material life, such as clothing and food. To determine answers, scholars must supplement archaeological data with information from colonial and other written sources who recorded daily life in the Yucatán, but since these documents are necessarily several centuries older than the apex of Uxmal's influence in the late 800s, they also have to be taken with a grain of salt.

Mayan elites, from the days of the Classical cities all the way down tot he arrival of the Spanish, delighted in adorning themselves in spectacular costumes, at least for ceremonial occasions. Early in the Classical Period, a royal "costume" was created, and it remained remarkably stable over the centuries, which in some sense is not surprising since European monarchs' ceremonial outfits have also not significantly altered in centuries and are in turn based off of models from the Roman Empire. The only good image of a monarch in Uxmal is of the famed Lord Chak on stela 14 (which is also discussed further below). In this image, he is dressed as a traditional Classical monarch, with an elaborate feathered headdress, a straight piercing through his nose, decorative plates in his ears, a collar made of jade, embroidered loincloth, and relatively simple sandals.[15] This shows that despite the dramatic changes the leaders of Uxmal made to their political system over time, they still maintained at least a symbolic connection to the ritual life of the Classical Maya courts.

15 Detail of Stela 14 can be found here:
   https://www.peabody.harvard.edu/CMHI/detail.php?num=14&site=Uxmal&type=Stela#

A depiction of Lord Chak

**Stela 14**

Outside of this very specific costume, clothing was probably quite simple, and the Spanish missionary Diego de Landa described the peasants as wearing clothing well-suited to the muggy climate of the region. Men wore a breechcloth, which consisted of a strip of cotton passing between the legs and pulled up through a cotton belt so that the ends dangled down in front of the groin and covered the buttocks. Mayan women (then and now) wore *huipil* - simple cotton gowns[16] - and square cotton mantles with holes cut in the center. On their feet, both genders and all social classes from the king down wore sandals made of deerskin or hemp with a thong between the toes.[17]

---

16 "The Huipil" at *Images of the Maya*. Accessed online at: http://www.flmnh.ufl.edu/maya/maya5.htm

Naturally, while clothing types were fairly uniform, there was plenty of variations and different styles. To begin with, the cotton garments - the breechcloths, huipils and mantles - were often elaborately decorated with embroidery, and the breechcloths could be adorned with colorful feathers that were also valuable trade goods. Elites adorned themselves with elaborate jewelry of jade, turquoise, shell and metal.

In addition to the relatively simple clothing, the people engaged in a number of forms of body modification for the purposes of beauty, including tattoos, filed teeth, piercings (especially of the nasal septum and the ears), and "coiffures as fine as those of the most coquettish Spanish women."[18] In addition to de Landa's rich descriptions, scholars can confirm these details thanks to fresco paintings from the walls of the ruins, carvings of both lordly individuals and their servitors on Stone, and a handful of painted paper books.

Clothing may have served an additional purpose beyond demonstrating one's good taste and social class (or lack thereof). For example, it may have also indicated one's place of origin. In the grand Guatemalan Maya market town of Chichicastenango, and even today in each of the surrounding Maya vilages, the women possess a style of huipil decoration that is unique to that community, marking individuals when they come to mix in the central community (as they would have in the markets of Uxmal).[19]

These markets would have been one of the primary reasons for the existence of Uxmal, in addition to its religious and political roles. Archaeologists have discovered that by the time of the founding of Uxmal, the Maya region had already been tied into a massive trade network for centuries. To the south, it extended into the rainforests of modern-day Honduras, but to the north it stretched all the way through today's Mexico into the American states of Arizona, New Mexico, Texas, and even Colorado and Utah. Long-distance trade goods that regularly passed hands included cotton, salt, cacao beans, jade, turquoise, polished silver mirrors, copper bells, seashells, colorful feathers, tine stone tools, and exceptional pottery. Locally, Uxmal would have served as the nexus for a much more localized network that brought goods in from the nearby farms and forests, including corn, beans, squash, chilis, fruit, wild game, turkeys, wild honey and wax, wood for fires and buildings, and other building materials[20]. The diet in Uxmal would have been heavy in corn, especially in the form of omnipresent tortillas, and relatively poor in protein despite the consumption of beans and wild game (especially deer)[21].

The Maya did not have permanent markets like the bazaars and souqs of the Muslim world, but

---

17 *Yucatan Before and After the Conquest* by Friar Diego de Landa. William Gates (trans.) 1566 (1978). Dover Books. Pgs 33, 53-54
18 de Landa 1566 (1978). Pgs 33, 53-54
19 *Chichicastenango: A Guatemalan Village* by Ruth Leah Bunzel (1967). University of Washington Press.
20 "Mesoamerican Plants and Foods" accessed online at:
   http://clio.missouristate.edu/chuchiak/New%20Webpage%20Images/HST%20397---Theme%205---Mesoamerican_plants_and_foods.htm
21 de Landa 1566 (1978). Pgs 32-39, 93-101

it appears that markets were regularly organized by urban elites in central plazas. In fact, the Maya word for plaza, k'iwik, is also the term used for a marketplace. Vendors, both local and long-distance, would have gathered in these central places and paid a fee to the city administration, and in turn, these fees and the tribute that elites took from their landholdings in surrounding communities formed the backbone of the elaborate elite lifestyle.

As the city grew in importance, the leaders increasingly connected it to surrounding communities via raised highways. Both the marketplaces and the highways were increasingly more extensive and formalized by the period of Uxmal's dominance over the region, prefiguring the continent-spanning trade network of Chichén Itzá.[22] Unlike Chichén Itzá, which would specialize in the export of first salt and then cotton, economic life in the city of Uxmal was not so specialized; instead, it tended to import primarily goods for elite consumption and a few for practical uses. For instance, obsidian for tools was probably imported in a raw form and then locally shaped to meet the needs of customers. Uxmal also served as a spot for redistribution, and its exports were most likely of the generalized southern Mesoamerican variety, including colorful feathers, cotton, and cacao.

## Chapter 3: Origins of the City

**Picture of a facade referred to as the Patio of the Birds**

---

22 "The Elusive Maya Marketplace: An Archaeological Consideration of the Evidence" by Leslie C. Shaw (2012) in *The Journal of Archaeological Research* January 2012. Accessed online at: http://link.springer.com.libezproxy2.syr.edu/article/10.1007/s10814-011-9055-0/fulltext.html

**Picture of the House of the Doves taken from the Great Pyramid**

Mayan civilization did not originate in Uxmal or anywhere near the now-venerable city. Instead, the Mayan peoples originated in the south, in the region that is now known as the Highlands of Guatemala, Belize and the Mexican states of Chiapas and Campeche. These wet and mountainous lands gave birth to a collection of complex, large, and perpetually feuding city-states like Tikal, Caracol, Calakmul and Palenque. The inhabitants of these cities, known as the Classic Maya people, thrived from roughly 200-800 AD, and they built mighty temples and established elaborate mythology, astronomy, architecture, irrigation and other arts and sciences[23].

However, by the 700s, the Classical Mayan society was beginning to suffer an ecological, political and demographic decline. Agriculture had always been relatively precarious, if only because their central staple of corn (maize) is por in proteins compared to other cereals and they had few domesticated animals to supplement their diet. Furthermore, humidity prevented easy storage of corn from season to season. When the Mayan populations peaked in the early 700s,

23 *The Atlas of World Archaeology* by Paul G. Bahn (ed.) (2009). The Brown Reference Group Ltd. Pgs 170-171.

desperate peasant farmers began cutting down hillside forests to grow more crops, but that led to widespread erosion and flooding. In 760, a devastating four decade-long drought hit the region, wiping out the food supply for all of the marginalized populations clinging to the hillsides. Exactly how this collapse occurred varied from place to place, but it would have been a gradual affair that witnessed the abandonment of eroded farms, the flooding of cities with beggars and work-seekers, and increasingly desparate monarchies starting wars over resources with their neighbors. Of course, the warfare would've led to more poor people in the cities in the form of refugees. Finally, there were urban revolts such as the one in 850 in Copan, where the royal palace was burnt. The political order then crumbled into bandit-kings pretending to be monarchs, and they would've been ruling over crumbling cities that suffered from widespread starvation, declining birthrates, shortened lifespans, and overall decline.[24]

Thanks to at least some if not all these factors, sometime in the 8th century AD, groups of farmers from the mountainous heartland of Mayan civilization began to slowly migrate north into the Yucatán Peninsula between the modern cities of Mérida and Cancún as they fled the crumbling kingdoms. Unlike the mighty dynasties of the great city-states that they left, noone felt the need to write about these people, perhaps because they were most likely economic or political refugees escaping the slow-moving crisis of the Classical Collapse. Their descendants today still live in the Yucatán and speak a language called Yucatecan Mayan, whose closest cousin is a relatively obscure Mayan language called Lacandón, which in turn is spoken by some of the poorest and most marginalized Mayan peasants living in today's state of Chiapas near the ruins of the Classical cities of Bonampak, Yaxchilan and Palenque[25]. Hence, one might suspect that at least the first or most numerous of the migrants heading north and carving settlements out of the Yucatán Jungle would have originated in this corner of the Mayan Highlands. Certainly, their agricultural experiences in the similar landscape of the Lacandon Jungle would have at least given them the hope that they might survive in their new homes.

Anyone seeking the originators of Uxmal and the entire Yucatecan Mayan cultural tradition (including the cities of Mayapán and Chichén Itzá) should look first to these humble migrants, who probably moved in groups larger than a single family. While one must be careful comparing groups spread across almost a thousand years, Mayans in both the Yucatán and Lacandon regions have demonstrated a remarkable sense of community spirit, including migrating as whole villages to escape oppressive governments[26], fighting guerilla wars in both the 19th and 20th centuries[27], and founding a region of semi-independent "Autonomous Villages" completely free of government control during the Zapatista Revolt from 1992 to today[28].

---

24 *Collapse: How Societies Choose to Fail or Succeed* (2005) by Jared Diamond. Pgs 164-5
25 "Maya, Yucatec" and "Lacandon" at the *Ethnologue, Languages of the World* website. Accessed online at: http://www.ethnologue.com/language/yua and http://www.ethnologue.com/language/lac.
26 Such as the village of Cobá described in: *Life Under the Tropical Canopy: Tradition and Change Among the Yucatec Maya* by Ellen Kintz (1990). Case Studies in Cultural Anthropology.
27 Especially the recent Zapatista Revolution and the brutal Caste War of 1847-1855: *The Caste War of the Yucatán* by Nelson A. Reed (2001). Stanford University Press.

Thus, while it can never be said for certain, it is probable that villages of peasants from the scarred and dying landscape around Palenque and Yaxchilan decided in their village councils to leave the rule of the Classical dynastic kings and to move to a harsh land to the north to settle new villages. Given enough time, they may have sent scouts ahead to find potential places to inhabit, or perhaps their decisions were made in a time of immediate crisis without the luxury of caution, but either way, they packed up their possessions in the 7th and 8th centuries and dropped out of the official Mayan written histories of the day, at least for a time.

What did they encounter as they moved north? While the Yucatán appears to the casual observer to be a lush rainforest covered in a thick, green forest cover, Mayan farmers would've considered the terrain to be as challenging and intimidating as a desert. If anything, it can be thought of as a "Green Desert" because it has little rainfall and almost no surface bodies of water. On top of that, the entire Yucatán Peninsula is a great sheet of limestone, so the water that does fall is either absorbed by plants or drains away immediately into the porous, cave-filled rocks under the thin soils. This landscape is known by geologists as a "karst topography." Like most rainforests, the soils of the Yucatán were poor because most of the nutrients were locked up within the trees themselves. Accustomed to the terraces and irrigated landscapes of the south, this Green Desert would have been as intimating to the migrants as any desert of sand and rock.

Eventually, the descendants of these migrants would spread out across the lowlands and found great cities on the limestone shelf, but the first migrants would have only been able to settle these regions in small, scattered groups. In the beginning, they had no way of yet knowing how to extract water from the underground sinkholes called cenotes, and it probably took several generations to breed new strains of corn and other crops more tolerant to the hostile conditions.

As a result, this first wave of inhabitants settled in the only area of notable topographic relief in the entire region: a line of low rises called the Puuc Hills. The term "Puuc" is derived from the Mayan word for a mountain ridge, and the region sprawls over 4,700 square miles (7,500 square kilometers). In the Puuc Region, they found grottoes, which were former sinkholes that had partially collapsed and thereby created open waterholes. These would later be supplemented by cutting cisterns called chultunes into the limestone rock. In this location, the settlers were able to recreate their dense southern villages, which would eventually become the nucleus of new cities, the most important of which would become Uxmal. The agricultural importance of the region would remain for centuries, and even the Spanish refered to it as the "granary" of their colony since it produced two crops of corn a year[29].

28 *Mayan Lives, Mayan Utopias: The Indigenous Peoples of Chiapas and the Zapatista Rebellion* by Jan Rus, Rosalva Aida Hernandez Castillo and Shannan L. Mattiace (eds.) (2003). Rowman and Littlefield.
29 Pohl (1999). Pgs 105 - 108

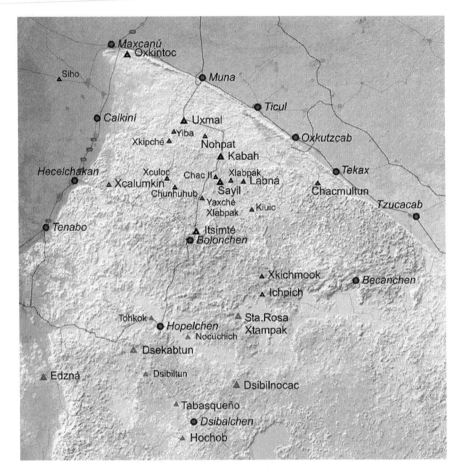

**A map of Mayan sites in the Puuc region**

It seems strange to many modern observers and scholars that the south collapsed while the north did not, especially considering the fact that agriculture in the south was richer and more stable than in the north. However, it was in the places where urban life was the most stable, the oldest, and the most secure that the collapse occurred. Meanwhile, in the frontier cities of the Puuc region - Uxmal foremost among them - Mayan urban life continued unabated for centuries to come. How can anyone explain this apparent paradox of famine in the rich lands and survival (if not feast) in the poor ones? In his book *Collapse: How Societies Choose to Fail or Succeed*, author Jared Diamond took up just this question, and he asserted that there are a number of causes. The first is that populations were much denser in the old kingdoms of the south, so farmers were forced to use even the most marginal of lands for the their crops, making them particularly susceptible to crop failure. Furthermore, the southern lands - unlike the Yucatán - had very deep water tables, making well-drilling impractical.[30] At the same time, the economies of these cities were largely isolated from easy water transport since they were in the Highlands, and trade was specialized around importing elite goods for the glorification of the dynastic system. The Yucatán, on the other hand, was not bound to the Dynastic system and was close to trade routes (especially the ascendent Chichén Itzá), and furthermore, the people here were willing to export bulk goods and import food during times of crisis. Together, these circumstances allowed the young Puuc cities to weather the storm of the Maya Collapse.

## Chapter 4: The Puuc Era

If a casual reader should learn anything about Uxmal compared to other Mayan ruins, it is that Uxmal was the creator and pinnacle of the uniquely Puuc Style. The Puuc style is definitely a Mayan form of architecture, but it changed many of the earlier techniques and assumptions. As discussed earlier, the city's emphasis moved from veneration of royal tombs in the Classical tradition to the creation of palaces for the living in the Puuc Style. Another major change was in decoration itself. Both northern and southern traditions involved the creation of elaborate facades, but while in the south these facades were constructed by shaping stucco on bare rock, in Uxmal (and its imitators), the facades were created by having artisans shape thousands of small geometric stole tiles that were then affixed to the exterior of the buildings, thus creating elaborate patterns[31].

30 Diamond (2005). Pgs 157 - 177
31 Pohl (1999). Pg 106

**Mosaic-like decorations on the Nunnery Quadrangle**

Puuc buildings were defined by having facades divided into plain, smooth lower portions and elaborately decorated friezes. These friezes were decorated with both geometric motifs but also masks of deities, especially the rain god Chak. In addition to Uxmal, where the style reached its pinnacle in the House of the Governor, it was also present in nearby Puuc cities like Kabah, Labna, and Sayil. The style is also present in the older areas of Chichén Itzá, such as the Nunnery Annex (no connection to the Nunnery Quadrangle in Uxmal) and the early forms of the Castillo pyramid[32].

A strong argument can be made that one of the ways that Uxmal broke most impressively from the Classical Tradition was its rejection of Dynasticism. Unlike its southern predecessors, which Uxmal copied so diligently in other matters, Uxmal did not maintain monuments designed to elevate and venerate a ruling dynasty; there are no great temples to royal lines (like the North Acropolis of Tikal) or elaborate carved stelae detailing royal pedigrees and the acts of kings. The House of the Governor was apparently a place of government, but it was not a royal palace, and the city had a number of elite compounds that must have been inhabited by rival families. This rule by council was referred to later during the League of the Mayapán and early Colonial

32 "Uxmal" at the *Encyclopedia Britannic Online.* Accessed online at:
   http://www.britannica.com/EBchecked/topic/620988/Uxmal#ref225522

period as "Mul Tepal" ("joint rule"). Officially, the city records do note a founder of the city, Hun-Uitzil-Chac, but nothing else is known about him besides his name, and it may be that he was created by elite families at a much later date[33].

There is some echo of this Mul Tepal system at Uxmal in a folktale recorded in the 19th century and known as the "Legend of the Dwarf." The story goes that an old woman hatched a magical egg and found a baby human within, but the child never grew to adult size and instead remained a dwarf. Dwarves hold a special place in Mesoamerican myth as figures blending the boundary between the human and supernatural worlds, so the adopted mother of this dwarf insisted that he should become king. The dwarf was forced into a physical challenge against the king, but when the dwarf triumphed, the angry sovereign insisted that the dwarf build the mightiest structure in the city overnight or be put to death. The next morning, the city was awed by the construction of the Pyramid of the Magician (also called the Pyramid of the Dwarf). The dwarf then killed the king and ascended to the throne.[34]

While the Pyramid of the Magician was definitely not built overnight and was constructed in a series of ever-greater stages, the story may explain the struggles for power in the great city. In the Classic Mayan city-state, the very idea that someone could challenge the king for his throne was never considered, and while there were certainly struggles, they were between members of existing dynastic lines and were never formalized or ritualized. In Uxmal, however, there may have been something like a confederation of elite families who competed for the rulership position. This was not a Classical royal tradition but may have emerged out of the more humble roots of Uxmal and other Puuc settlements, and the relative egalitarianism of the peasant communities from which they came.

That said, by the time Uxmal became a proper city, any signs of this egalitarianism were purely vestigial. Instead, it may have been that Uxmal from the 750s on could be compared to the Roman Republic under the early Caesars: officially a republic with a nod towards the common citizenry, but in practice an elected monarchy dominated by the powerful elite patricians in the capital city.

From this period of glory and power emerges a single name. In fact, it is the only name of a monarch at Uxmal (aside from the name of the founder) that has survived in the written record: Chan Chak K'ak'nal Ajaw, more commonly referred to in the modern era as "Lord Chak." Lord Chak ascended to the double-headed jaguar throne of Uxmal (in fact, scholars have found an image of him atop the throne) in approximately 875 and ruled until 910. Under Lord Chak, the city rose from being one of many amongst the rival hill towns of the Puuc to the undisputed,

33 "Lords of the Northern Maya: Dynastic History in the Inscriptions of Uxmal and Chichén Itza" by Jeff Karl Kowalski in *Expedition Magazine*. Vol 27 No 3 November 1985. Accessed online at: http://www.penn.museum/sites/expedition/lords-of-the-northern-maya/
34 The tale is recounted at greater length in: *The Myths of Mexico and Peru* by Lewis Spence. 1913 (2005). Barnes and Noble Books. Pgs 167 - 168

preeminent political power. During this period, the current forms of both the Nunnery Quadrangle and the Temple of the Magician were created, and the House of the Governor and main ballcourt were entirely constructed. Based off of inscriptions in other settlements, it appears that Lord Chak led his city's armies to victory as well, including conquering neighboring Kabah and constructing an impressive 11 kilometer highway connecting the two.

Another surviving inscription notes his ancestry. According to that record, Lord Chaak Uinal Kan and Lady "Bone" were his parents, but there is no indication either way as to whether Lord Chaak Uinal Kan also held the double-headed jaguar throne. It may be that his mother came from a noble family in Chichén Itzá (which was on the rise in this period) as there is an allusion to that city in conjunction with her name, but its exact meaning is obscure. That said, alliances cemented by marriage in this way were not uncommon amongst elites and it may have been one of the reasons why he was able to consolidate power[35].

Lord Chak's reign is significant not only for Uxmal - it was undoubtedly the moment of greatest glory for the city - but for the Mayan world in general. By the time of his death in 910 AD, all of the great Classical cities had fallen. The last monument was erected in Tikal in 889 AD, the royal palace of Copan was burned in 850 AD, Dos Pilas had been turned into an armed camp for a bandit lord, and Palenque had been quiet for over a century[36]. The stelae erected to commemorate Lord Chak are the very last monuments to a true Classic Maya King, so his death serves as the end of the Classic Era. Of course, that's not to say Uxmal disappeared, but it did become subservient for an extended period of time as it lived within the shadow of Chichén Itzá to the north. The last construction within the ceremonial center of Uxmal was finished by 925 AD.[37]

The seeming lack of kings in the record for Uxmal has led some to believe that the city was actually ruled by its most commonly depicted figure: the rain god Chaac (also spelled Chaak, Chac, and Chak). In fact, it's imposible to discuss the Puuc style without referring to the omnipresent Chaac masks dotting horizontal surfaces, and the god's image is quite distinctive; he has "goggle" eyes, a proboscus-like nose and often a gaping toothy maw for a mouth[38].

35 Kowalski (1985)
36 For more on the Collapse from a southern perspective, consult *Tikal: The History of the Ancient Maya's Famous Capital* by Jesse Harasta (2014). Charles Rivers Editors.
37 *The Chronicle of the Mayan Kings and Queens: Deciphering the Dynasties of the Ancient Maya* by Simon Martin and Nikolai Grube (2000). Thames and Hudson. Pgs 227
38 For example: http://www.flickr.com/photos/tom_martin/4151711134/

*Effigy urn in the form of*
*Chac, the Rain God*

**A figurine depicting Chaac**

Chaac is an old god that was brought up to the Yucatán with the earliest migrants, but the origins of the deity during the Classic Era are up for debate. It has been argued that Chaac was originally brought to the Mayan lands by invaders from Teotihuacán near what is today Mexico City. Teotihuacán conquered Tikal and other Highland cities in the 4th century, and the city worshipped a similar god named Tlaloc. In turn, Tlaloc may have come from a fang-mouthed, wide-eyed rain deity called the "Baby Jaguar" by archaeologists and worshiped among the Olmec people of Veracruz as early as 1500 BC[39]. Chaac was therefore a god of antiquity who held powerful resonance with the Maya by the time they built the city of Uxmal, and it is not surprising in a city whose agriculture depended so much upon regular rainfall (and in a region experiencing prolonged drought) that they would make this deity preeminent in their religious rites.[40]

## Chapter 5: Chichén Itzá and the Eclipse of Uxmal

Uxmal's time at the top was relatively short-lived. After the death of Lord Chak, the city was not abandoned like so many of the southern cities, but it went into a long period of inactivity. No new monumental buildings were constructed, no kings were commemorated, and the city does not appear to be mentioned in the inscriptions of its neighbors.

The new power in the region was Chichén Itzá, a lowland city that took advantage of several deep natural wells called cenotes and a monopoly on local salt production. Originally a tiny Mayan statelet surviving in obscurity for several centuries, it was only after the collapse of Classical Mayan society that Chichén Itzá exploded onto the scene. Leveraging its salt production, it was able to command wealthy trade routes connecting it to the Toltec Empire in central Mexico. While Uxmal dominated the central Puuc interior, the Itzaes of Chichén looked outwards to the sea.

It is possible that the two were allies in the early period, as there is evidence that Lord Chak's mother was associated with Chichén, and there is no evidence that Chichén Itzá's rise was accompanied with conflict with Uxmal, a common event when one Mayan city displaced another. Moreover, early buildings in Chichén seem to be modeled after Uxmal. Thus, it's possible that after 925, Uxmal became a sort of junior partner, with its increasingly venerable buildings and its firm dedication to the worship of Chaac[41].

39 *Teotihuacan: The History of Ancient Mesoamerica's Largest City* by Jesse Harasta (2014). Charles Rivers Editors.
40 "Chac" at the *Encyclopedia Mythica* by Henk Jan van Scheicoven (1997). Accessed online at: http://www.pantheon.org/articles/c/chac.html and "Chac" at the *Mythology Dictionary* (2012). Accessed online at: http://www.mythologydictionary.com/chac-mythology.html
41 *Chichén Itza: The History and Mystery of the Maya's Most Famous City* by Jesse Harasta (2013). Charles Rivers Editors.

Either way, the situation fundamentally changed in the late 9th century and early 10th century, the period in which the elites of Chichén Itzá adopted cultural traditions imported from the non-Mayan Toltec Empire (located in today's Central Mexico). The most obvious change that can be found today is in the architectural style, because the main Puuc pyramid was covered in a new layer entirely based off of Toltec designs. Chichén Itzá also seems to have imported Toltec warrior societies, a central part of the Toltec state, as well as the worship of the god Kukulcán. There is an alternative theory that the Toltecs conquered the Yucatán, but there is no hard evidence for conquest like there was for Teotihuacan's conquest of Tikal, so it has been largely discarded.[42]

Regardless, thanks to the adoption of Toltec cultural elements, the elites of the newly cosmopolitan system appear to have turned their back on Mayan tradition and instead adopted what may have been viewed as a prestigious international cultura, one associated with exotic goods, wealth, and fascinating new religious ideas. This may have been similar to the ways that European courts far from Paris adopted the French language and culture during the 18th century in order to relate to the standards of international elite high society.

At the heart of the new culture was the cult of the Sovereign Feathered Serpent, a pan-Mesoamerican god called Kukulcán among the Maya and Quetzalcoatl in Central Mexico. Considered to be both a creator deity who protected the world and gave humanity the gift of civilization and also a messianic man who came to Earth and was driven away by a depraved sorcerer, his story resonated all throughout today's Mexico. Its original cultic center was the Toltec capital of Tula, but eventually, Chichén became an alternative center for worship and pilgrimage, making it the heart of the new religion.

42 "Kukulkan" and "Quetzalcoatl" at the *Encyclopedia Mythica*. Accessed online at: http://www.pantheon.org/.
   "Kukulcan" at the *Mythology Dictionary*. Accessed online at: http://www.mythologydictionary.com/kukulcan-mythology.html

**A depiction of the deity on El Castillo at Chichén Itzá**

There is some evidence of the cult of Kukulcán in Uxmal as well. The feathered serpent appears carved in the friezes of the Nunnery Quadrangle, which was built during the reign of Lord Chak, but the deity never had the importance he did at Chichén. Just as Uxmal is the city of Chaac - his face is everywhere and the city's greatest king took his name - Chichén came to be associated with Kukulcán. At the same time, the cult of Chaac appears to have been eclipsed in the hearts of the Maya by the new religion, though this does not mean that the faith in Chaac disappeared entirely. Mayan polytheism allows for the worship of numerous gods, so Chaac may have merely taken a backseat to Kukulcán. At the same time, it's possible that formerly ascendant priests of the rain god were bitter about their new position and sought to knock Kukulcán from his pedestal.

## Chapter 6: Revolution and The League of Mayapán

In roughly 1179, the Chichén sister-city of Tula in the Toltec homeland was sacked by invaders from the north, as was the northern port city of el Tajín,[43] which had linked the two. In essence, the trade routes that sustained Chichén power were severed. Already pressured by these losses, the ruling Itzá clan of Chichén Itzá apparently began to apply greater economic pressure on their subject peoples, perhaps to acquire food reserves during crises, perhaps to defend their

---

43 The Huaxtecs who had built el Tajín and bridged the Tula-Chichén gap were located in central Mexico but were ethnically and linguistically related to the Maya.

borders against now-forgotten enemies, or perhaps to just maintain their luxurious lifestyles. The effect, however, was a greater presence of ostensibly foreign and increasingly despised mercenaries in the streets of the city. These "mercenaries" may have been Toltec refugees staying with their fellow co-religionists and members of the same warrior societies, or they may have been literal mercenaries brought in.

Either way, the stage was set for revolt, and the revolution came in the form of a remarkable figure named Hunac Ceel. A military general and presumably member of an elite family from the interior town of Telchaquillo, Hunac Ceel attempted to overthrow the Itzá Dynasty using forces from the inside. His first attempt, probably in the early 1200s, was completely unsuccessful, and after his army was shattered, he was captured. It was determined by the city's leaders, including the ruling Itzá Ah Mex K'uuk, that he should be put to death, so he was sacrificed as an offering to Chaak and thrown into the city's Sacred Cenote well, which was dedicated to the rain god. To everyone's surprise, however, Hunac Ceel emerged alive the next day with prophecies he claimed were from Chaak, and when his prophecies came true, Ah Mex K'uuk (fearing his power) sent him back into the interior to rule over a peripheral town. Hunac Ceel traveled through the old Puuc heartland and gathered strength until he led a second attack on Chichén Itza. This time he was successful in defeating the Itzaes, and he drove the survivors into present-day Guatemala. After taking out Chichén Itzá, he established a new capital for his revolutionary government (the "League") at the town of Mayapán.[44]

Of course, as the fantastic nature of the story suggests, there is plenty of debate over the actual nature of this revolution. It is tempting to see it as a form of nationalism on the part of the Maya, who finally had the opportunity to overthrow hated foreign rulers and establish a true Mayan government again. Folktales, however, paint a picture of inter-elite strife, so all kinds of alternate theories have been thrown about. Perhaps an unnamed Mayan prince (Hunac Ceel?) was spurned for the hand of the daughter of the ruler of Chichén (Ah Mex K'uuk?), so the prince then led an army that captures his beloved and destroys her home city.

Either way, the inhabitants of Mayapán were able to form an inter-city Mul Tepal (joint rule), with elite families from all of the rebellious cities coming together in council in the new city. Mayapán was therefore not a center of international trade like Chichén had been but instead a planned political capital (akin to modern-day Washington D.C.) with mansions for each of the families for when they came to court. The descendants of Hunac Ceel were known as the Cocom dynasty, and when the Spanish arrived, they still ruled over a small kingdom based around the town of Sotuta between the ruins of Mayapán and Chichén Itza.

The Cocom were not, however, the only prominent family within the League, though they may have had a permanent ceremonial position at its head. At the time of Spanish colonization, the

---

44 "Chapter 2: The Rise of Hunac Ceel to Power" from the *Chilam Balam* accessed online at: http://www.bibliotecapleyades.net/chilam_balam/cbc07.htm

League had broken down and a full 16 petty kingdoms had been formed out of its ruins, so it's possible there had been at least that many powerful families represented at the League. The most important, however, were the Xiu (also called the Tutul Xiu), who were the rulers of Uxmal.

The exact origins of the Xiu are a bit vague, but the family has maintained a genealogical chart since ancient times that claims to include Hun-Uitzil-Chac, the mythical founder of Uxmal. Of course, the fact that they assert this blood connection, while interesting sociologically, hardly confirms its veracity. It's far more likely that this connection was invented by later generations to justify power that they had already seized.[45] What is known is that by the time of Hunac Ceel's rise, the Xiu were firmly in power in Uxmal and that they apparently delivered the city to the League. Their participation, both for material and symbolic purposes, was so crucial that it appears they were granted the status of the League's second family[46].

The new order established by Hunac Ceel and his the Xiu allies appears to not only have displaced Chichén Itza,but also the Toltec-infused cultural order they created. For instance, archaeologists have noted that the previously-popular Toltec style pottery was replaced by self-consciously traditional Mayan styles that had long been out of style.[47] There may have been a religious dimension to this change as well. On the one hand, the worship of Kukulcán did not cease; in fact, the high priest of the god was merely taken from Chichén and moved to a new pyramid at Mayapán (a smaller version of the Castillo pyramid), where he continued to preside as before[48]. At the same time, however, there appears to have been a religious dimension to the revolt since Hunac Ceel received his prophetic visions from Chaak, he traveled to Chaak's city (Uxmal) for support, and there was a general revival of Chaak worship. Unlike the worship of Kukulcán, the worship of Chaak has continued to this day amongst Yucatecan peasants.

Eventually, like the power structures before it, the League was shattered, and the Spanish missionary Diego de Landa described the situation roughly three centuries later: "The governing Cocom began to covet riches, and to that end negotiated with the garrison kept by the kings of Mexico in Tabasco and Xicalango, that he would put the city in their charge. In this way he introduced the Mexicans into Mayapán, oppressed the poor and made slaves of many."[49]

This may sound like a repeat of the fall of Chichén, but there are differences. First, Mayapán never dominated the Yucatan economically or religiously in the way that Chichén did; the Cocom may have desired power in the manner that the Itzaes had, but they appear to have always feared for their strength. In addition to possibly using mercenaries, the Cocom built thick walls

---

45 Kowalski (1985)

46 *Mayapán: History of the Mayan Capital* by Jesse Harasta (2014). Charles Rivers Editors.

47 "Survival and Revival of Terminal Classic Traditions at Postclassic Mayapán" by Susan Milbrath and Carlos Peraza Lope (2009). In the journal *Latin American Antiquity* 20(4) 581-606 accessed online at: http://www.jstor.org/discover/10.2307/40650048?uid=3739832&uid=2&uid=4&uid=3739256&sid=2110326328 1091

48 de Landa 1566 (1978). Pgs 10 - 11

49 de Landa 1566 (1978). Pg 15-16

around Mayapán. No Mayan city had been walled like that before, leading historians to assume that the Cocom felt particularly vulnerable in their capital. This was apparently for good reason, because Landa - who it must be said was a close ally of the Xius - noted that "the lord of the Tutul-xiu never gave his consent to [the mercenaries]... the chiefs then attached themselves to the party of Tutul-xiu, a man patriotic like his ancestors, and they plotted to kill Cocom. This they did, killing at the same time all of his sons save one who was absent...[50]" This probably occurred around 1450 AD.

Perhaps the Xiu had hoped that after the fall of the Cocom, they would be able to ascend to power in the League, but if so, they were sorely disappointed. The League was shattered forever, and the leaders of the revolution soon retreated back to their own seats of power and began warring against one another. Furthermore, it was during this period that Uxmal was finally abandoned. It's not entirely clear why, but all over the northern Yucatan at this point, the great cities were in terminal decline, including Uxmal, Mayapán, and Chichén Itzá. The civil wars may have brought long-distance trade, the lifeblood of many cities, to a halt and may have disrupted local food supplies. Armies may have looted settlements and commoners may have fled to the fortified strongholds of their lords. The fortification of Mayapán may have signified that this internal warring may have begun long before the official collapse of the League.

Whatever the case, the Xiu family left Uxmal to settle in the town of Maní, which was located east of Uxmal in the foothills of the Puuc region. The Xius continued to rule over Uxmal's old heartland, including the city itself, Kabah, Sayil, Labna, and the other ancient Puuc towns[51]. Indeed, the Xiu continued regular religious pilgrimage to Uxmal and recognized it as their ancient seat of power, but the Mayan world had permanently shifted, and Uxmal – while still revered – was never again permanently inhabited.

## Chapter 7: The Abandonment and Rediscovery of Uxmal

Uxmal remained revered among the Maya, but everything changed in 1521 when Hernan Cortes landed on the Yucatan peninsula. While Cortes would not tarry - he had an Aztec Empire to conquer - he was only the first conquistador to arrive in the region, and the Spanish established settlements on the coast and invaded the Yucatan in 1528 and again in 1535. It was only in 1542 that they were successful, and that was because the canny Xiu in Maní decided to leverage the Spanish presence by making an alliance. This pact with the devil did aid the Xiu in the short term, as they were able to dominate local politics and re-create Mayan unity, but the last independent Yucatecan Dynasty fell in 1546.[52] Instead, the Maya were placed under the increasingly fanatical jurisdiction of the Bishop Diego de Landa, and in 1562, furious by what he saw as treasonous heresy from his own converts, de Landa collected all of the Maya books that he could get his hands on and burned them in the central plaza of Maní. He was quite successful

---

50 de Landa 1566 (1978). Pg 16
51 de Landa 1566 (1978). Pg 137
52 Martin and Grube (2000). Pgs 229-230

by his standards, since only three known Mayan texts survived.

After the Spanish takeover, the Xiu were converted to Catholicism and abandoned their rituals at Uxmal, but perhaps not all of their subjects were so willing because the Spanish would occasionally report finding incense and offerings in the ruined temples late into the colonial period. Throughout that period, occasional Spanish tourists would visit Uxmal, enough that the city was never completely forgotten by non-Maya but not enough to excite international interest.

The outside world only sat up and took interest because of the remarkable work of two English-speaking scholars: Catherwood and Stevens. Their text, *Incidents of Travel in Central America, Chiapas & Yucatán* (1843), was an international sensation and fit into a growing interest in lost cities in the West.[53][54] However, the region was not available for research throughout much of the 19th century because the Mayan Revolt and the brutal Caste War set the region aflame.[55]

That situation eventually changed, and in 1893, an archaeological team working in Uxmal from Harvard created casts of a number of the most prominent buildings, including facades of the House of the Governor. These casts were dismantled and shipped to Chicago, where they were reconstructed for the famed Chicago Columbian Exhibition (also known as the World's Fair or the "White City"). These facades were visited by thousands of spectators, including a number of American architects, one of whom was the innovative Frank Lloyd Wright. Wright subsequently adopted many Puuc-style elements - even including Chaak masks - into a number of his buildings. This style, called the Maya Revival, reached its zenith upon the construction of the Charles Ennis House and the Aline Barnsdall House[56].

Since that point, Uxmal has been simultaneously an archaeological and touristic destination, in part due to its remarkable architecture but also because of its accessibility to visitors who come to the town of Meridá. The Mexican government took a particular interest in its ancient heritage after the Mexican Revolution (which finished in 1920), and the ruins were declared patrimony of the state and given official protectors and interpreters. This status was further bolstered in 1996 after UNESCO recognized Uxmal as one of their World Heritage Sites, arguably the most prestigious award that can be given to an ancient site today.[57]

As a result, more than a millennium after it flourished, Uxmal is a remarkable mountain city that is visited and studied by multitudes around the world, and it is still treasured in the hearts of

53  "John Lloyd Stephens and Frederick Catherwood: Exploring the Land of the Maya" by Nicoletta Maestri. Accessed online at: http://archaeology.about.com/od/mayaresearchers/a/Stephens-and-Catherwood.htm
54  "Frederick Catherwood's Lithographs" accessed online at: http://www.casa-catherwood.com/catherwoodinenglish.html
55  *The Caste War of the Yucatán* by Nelson A. Reed (2001). Stanford University Press. Pg 154.
56  Pohl (1999). Pg 107
57  ""Pre-Hispanic Town of Uxmal" at the UNESCO World Heritage List, accessed online at: http://whc.unesco.org/en/list/791

Mayans and Mexicans in general. Furthermore, it continues to be gradually restored, with careful research leading to the rebuilding of important structures. Undoubtedly this continued work will give new insights in the coming years, and there is much still to learn about the beautiful and enigmatic ruins.

**19th century illustrations depicting Uxmal**

## Timeline of Events in the Yucatan Postclassic Period

| | |
|---|---|
| 455 AD | Foundation of the first settlement at Chichén Itzá (est.) |
| 750 AD | Foundation of the city of Uxmal (est.) |
| 750 - 900 AD | Collapse of the Classic Maya states in the south |
| 850 AD | Beginning of the Puuc Style (est.) |
| 875-900 AD | The Reign of Lord Chaak in Uxmal |
| 875-880 AD | Height of the Puuc Style in the Yucatán |
| 925 AD | End of Royal Power in Uxmal<br>End of the Classic Mayan Period |
| Mid 900s | Completion of the last stage of Pyramid of the Magician in Uxmal |
| Late 900s | Chichén is the dominant power in the Yucatan, Uxmal eclipsed |
| Early 1000s | Chichén is ruled by Toltec-influenced Leaders |
| 1100s | First small settlements at Mayapán |
| 1179 | Fall of the Toltec city of Tula (est.) |
| Early 1200 | Foundation of Maní by the Xiu (est.) |
| 1221 | Hunac Ceel's Vision |
| 1222 | Hunac Ceel's Conquest of Chichén<br>Foundation of Mayapán as the Capital |
| 1441 | Fall of the Cocomes and the destruction of Mayapán, Uxmal begins final decline |
| 1521 | Cortes stops on the Mayan coast while traveling to Mexico |
| 1528 & 1535 | First and Second Spanish Invasion |
| 1542 | Spanish Conquest of Maní and the Xiu-Spanish Alliance |
| 1546 | Last Yucatecan cities fall to the Spanish |
| 1562 | The Great Auto-de-fé in Maní, destruction of the Mayan elite culture |
| 1840s | Catherwood and Steven visit Uxmal and other cities<br>The Maya led by the Cocomes and Itzaes rise up against Mexico |
| 1890s | Harvard University Expedition studies site and brings casts to 1893 Chicago World's Fair, exciting international attention |
| 1909 | Sylvanus Morley mapped Uxmal |
| 1975 | Inauguration of nightly Lights and Sound exhibition |
| 1996 | Inscription of the site onto the UNESCO World Heritage List |

## Bibliography

Dunning, Nicholas P. (2006). "Long twilight or new dawn? Transformation of Maya civilization in the Puuc region". In Nikolai Grube (ed.). Maya: Divine Kings of the Rain Forest. Eva Eggebrecht and Matthias Seidel (assistant eds.). Cologne, Germany: Könemann. pp. 323–337. ISBN 978-3-8331-1957-6. OCLC 71165439.

Restall, Matthew (1997). The Maya World. Yucatecan Culture and Society, 1550–1850. Stanford: Stanford University Press. ISBN 978-0-8047-3658-9.

Schele, Linda; and David Freidel (1992). A Forest of Kings: The Untold Story of the Ancient Maya (pbk reprint ed.). New York: Harper Perennial. ISBN 0-688-11204-8. OCLC 145324300.

Stephens, John L. (1841). Incidents of Travel in Central America, Chiapas, and Yucatan. in 2 vols. Frederick Catherwood (illus.). New York: Harper & Brothers. OCLC 863468

Wagner, Elizabeth (2006). "Maya Creation Myths and Cosmography". In Nikolai Grube (ed.). Maya: Divine Kings of the Rain Forest. Eva Eggebrecht and Matthias Seidel (Assistant eds.). Cologne: Könemann. pp. 280–293. ISBN 3-8331-1957-8. OCLC 71165439

25512281R00029

Made in the USA
Middletown, DE
01 November 2015